Do Build

How to make and lead
a business the world needs.

Alan Moore

Published by
The Do Book Company 2021
Works in Progress Publishing Ltd
thedobook.co

Text © Alan Moore 2021
Photography © Julian Calverley 2021
p88 © ON Power photo by Árni Sæberg

To find out more about our company,
books and authors, please visit
thedobook.co or follow us **@dobookco**

5 per cent of our proceeds from the sale
of this book is given to The Do Lectures
to help it achieve its aim of making
positive change: **thedolectures.com**

Cover designed by James Victore
Book designed and set by Ratiotype

Printed and bound by OZGraf Print
on Munken, an FSC® certified paper

MIX
Paper from
responsible sources
FSC® C163799

A CIP catalogue record for this book
is available from the British Library

ISBN 978-1-907974-91-5

10 9 8 7 6 5 4 3 2

Contents

For Liu Qian
Your way of smiling is a gift
bestowed upon this world

There is no wealth but life. Life, including all its powers of love, of joy, and of admiration. That country is the richest which nourishes the greatest numbers of noble and happy human beings; that man is richest, who, having perfected the functions of his own life to the utmost, has also the widest helpful influence, both personal, and by means of his possessions, over the lives of others.

John Ruskin

1
What does the world need?

Before it is too late, we should embark in earnest on the most fundamental existential (and also truly revolutionary) task facing modern civilisation, that of making any future growth compatible with the long-term preservation of the only biosphere we have.

—

Vaclav Smil

'What does the world need?' is one of the most pressing questions of our time. Why? Because this question encompasses a number of other questions: Why are we here? For what reason do we exist? What values create the foundation of what matters most? What kind of world are we trying to make? We must transform our mindset, but to what end?

The Coronavirus pandemic has brought us to a moment of transformation at great speed. It is a tragedy but one that offers an extraordinary space for us to reimagine what a better future might look like for us all.

Now is the moment of opportunity. Business can do good. To remake our world, it can seek the good and manifest it in all that we create. If we are to build a future worth living in, we must try to achieve equilibrium between our economy, our ecology and our community. We need a reimagining of the very purpose of business, and the role it plays in regenerating our economy, our environment and our civilisation. That is what the world needs from business. That is what business needs to give the world.

We must turn away from the devastating effects of the quest for endless growth, pursuing profit at any and all cost.

The universal virtue of doing good in business, combined with the need for a more life-changing and regenerative society, has been veiled for too long. We now stand on the edge: one third of the world's entire wealth is held in 'offshore' tax havens; we are beset by fires and floods; the glaciers are retreating from the mountains and calving themselves into the oceans at breakneck speed.

Your customers' needs have changed, too. For some time, a shift has been taking place in the discussion about what type of world we want to live in. This is fuelled by a generational shift in values, knowledge and understanding of how our world is not working for many people. Our children's generation has no ticket to the future. They won't have jobs for life. They won't have great returns on their pensions. Many of them know they won't ever be able to afford to buy a house. Yet, despite all of this, they are steeped in values. They may think a lot about the environment and be deeply concerned with matters of social responsibility, equality and diversity.

Today, in business, there is a growing realisation that we are counting the wrong things, which diminishes how we see the world. We have lost the sense of life as a whole, as wholesome. We must start by accepting the interconnectedness of our natural world, because nature is not designed selfishly, but to serve and support the needs of all life. We need to measure success in a more nurturing and qualitative way. We need to ask: what is growth, what is progress and how do we measure these things?

We could start by appreciating the accomplishments of our economic growth over the last 200 years, but also acknowledging its increasing limitations. We must change the means by which we measure productivity, prosperity, sustainability, profit and loss, and review the business models designed for endless growth. We need to measure carbon capture, regeneration and the quality of life.

I want to show you how you can deliver the equilibrium that the world needs. I have not drawn from the wishing well of 'make believe', but from the hard truth of people living in the real world, who demand positive and lasting change. They are ready to create, make and build that new reality. Perhaps it's only a matter of time before people go to Mars. But not everyone is going to Mars, so we might as well fix the planet we already have.

It has been a privilege to research this book, as I have spoken with so many wonderful people, all invested in building a better future. They are all in business in one form or another. Years of hard work have gone into creating these organisations, often against seemingly insurmountable odds. Yet the enduring benefits that they are collectively bringing can only be applauded. (Some might even deserve a standing ovation.)

No one is perfect. All these businesses are on a journey. They aspire to make the world a better place through their vision, leadership, culture, decision-making processes, governance, business models, products and services. It doesn't matter whether you are a small, a medium or a large business; you have an important role to play in creating a business the world needs.

The nineteenth-century critic and social thinker John Ruskin recognised our need to do more than satisfy our own desires. We need to focus on what will sustain us for eternity. What if we were to view what we make as gifts bestowed upon the world? Reflect on what type of world you are trying to make, build and create. Consider the social purpose of making, whether you are working for a vineyard, a bank, an energy company, a farm or a trainer brand. How does it matter to the world?

Be inspired. Feel the potential of your dreaming. Don't be overwhelmed. When we imagine the possibility of something, it has a chance of becoming a reality. Why have I selected the title *Do Build* for this book? Because you are a builder of a new way of living and working, creating a new business for a new age with a new vision.

The principles I share for business leaders, and the questions I ask about how we should design and build, are a calculated provocation and a guide to how to challenge our current mindset. There are many benefits of change. If you are just beginning your journey as a founder, or at a moment of rethinking the role of your business in today's world, take the time to ask yourself a few questions:

— What world am I trying to create?

— What will be my legacy and my company's legacy for future generations?

— What would my business look like if it were more beautiful?

— Why would I want to do it any other way?

These questions speak to our collective imagination. Your imagination is fired by suggestion, not by direction. It is in that leap of imaginative creativity, so compelling in its elegance, that you can bring a new reality into existence.

2
Building foundations

For anything to last, it needs strong foundations. For a business to continue giving value to the world, we must explore its life-giving properties. In order to do so, we need to move beyond the idea of sustainability to the idea of regeneration. One way for business to do good is by regenerating our economy, our environment and our civilisation. The foundations of business now and in the future must be premised on regeneration, creating the conditions for all of life to thrive. For me, these foundations must include beauty, nature, biomimicry, design, values and metrics, and governance.

Beauty

The human spirit needs beauty. It enriches us and lifts us up. Beauty is a felt knowledge, connecting us spiritually, intellectually, sensually and ethically to every part of our lives. It expresses the idea that we can seek the good and manifest it in all that we create in this world. What I have learned since writing *Do Design: Why beauty is key to everything*, is that the human spirit strives for more beauty. Beauty is good; it is a universal truth that beauty is a vital part of our DNA. As I wrote in *Do Design*, beautiful things are prepared with love and infused with optimism. They simply say life is, and can be, worthwhile. But how can beauty be a frame for business?

Peter Childs, who was the founding Head of the Dyson School of Design Engineering at Imperial College London, says beauty should be reclaimed by schools teaching business. He believes beauty offers a different way of framing our world: 'We talk about rationale, philosophies, aesthetics and ascetics. The concept of beauty tends to be reserved for the beauties of nature. Can we actually set out to do something beautiful? There is an aspiration worthy of aiming towards. Can we teach beautiful design, beautiful engineering? It is probably a bit like, can we teach subjects such as creativity?'

Childs goes on: 'Well, we can certainly augment creativity, and beauty would be a subject where one could augment and enhance what people are already doing, and I suspect with time actually lift the whole cohort, so that what they are doing in terms of their impact on society could truly be beautiful.'

In essence, beauty is a verb, 'I do.' It should be our frame for life.

Climeworks is an exemplar of Childs's suggestion that there is a cohort motivated to make a positive contribution to our world. Climate change is both a challenge and an opportunity. Ten billion tons of carbon dioxide needs to be removed from the air every year and stored. Simple maths, just a really big number. Climeworks technology extracts carbon dioxide directly from the atmosphere, and uses it to provide renewable energy or make carbonated beverages, or turns it into stone and stores it deep underground. The technology is pioneering and their business enables individuals as well as organisations to contribute to climate take back and carbon dioxide reduction through a subscription model. This is regenerative economics in practice.

Everlane also belongs to this cohort that is striving to find innovative ways of restoring equilibrium between our economy, our ecology and our community. The company sells sustainably sourced clothing. Founded in 2011, it has 1.5 million customers. 'Clothes should be built to last,' says the CEO of Everlane, Michael Preysman. 'The question for all other leaders out there is, what side of history do you want to be on? We have a belief you can be ethical and profitable.' The denim factory that makes its jeans recycles 98 per cent of its water (see *everlane.com*).

Nature

Nature is calling us, because we are part of nature. We belong to the natural world, because we are made from the same molecular material. This is not a romantic notion; there is evidence that demonstrates our relationship with nature is fundamental to our mental health and spiritual wellbeing — green spaces bring health benefits, for example. So, why wouldn't you protect the very thing from which you are made? According to Buddhist philosophy, our true nature is to be caring and kind. We need to see the bigger picture.

When introducing people to the beauty of nature, I ask them to shut their eyes and visualise themselves in a spaceship. Looking out of a window, they can see the sun, the earth and the moon, hanging in the endless void. Sitting next to them is the astronaut Edgar Mitchell, and he is saying that when he first saw our planet and the celestial bodies from space, he was overcome by a sense of wonder or euphoria that flowed through his body.

I ask them to imagine that Mitchell looks at them and says the molecules in his body and the molecules in this spaceship and in their body, are all forged in an ancient star: 'We are all stardust.' I go on to tell a story of how astronauts experience the 'Overview' effect. This is a cognitive shift where they are motivated by a deep need to protect the earth and serve humanity. They realise there are no borders, and we are one species. That earth is a tiny fragile planet, existing in the vast infinite entity that is space.

For a time, I let the silence fill the space of the room. I ask people to open their eyes. Resistance has dissipated. Instead, there is a pathway for me to speak about the joy that the natural world gives us, how it can foster wonder, and why we know we belong to its pure state.

I then ask this question: If we are all made of the same stuff, what is our role in this world and how do we act? This exercise is one I have delivered many times. To begin with, it is greeted with varying degrees of scepticism. But it is a means to reconnect people to nature. It is a way to reframe and understand our connection with the natural world, without which we can neither respect nor wish to protect our fragile earth.

Seeing the world as deeply interconnected is imperative, for the simple reason of understanding cause and effect. Since we are entangled in creation, it is vital for us to show care and respect for what we have. Without this deep reframing, we may struggle to meet design challenges and be less willing to seek transformative solutions to problems of manufacturing, architecture and resources. We could be less inclined to make creative leaps of the imagination in developing the products and services that this world needs.

Biomimicry

Nature is running one of the longest and most continuous Research and Development projects around. No company could ever afford such a long-term investigation into what makes life thrive. Moreover, nature works on the principle of regeneration, with a complex ecosystem that supports all of life. It makes sense to learn from the gift of nature, as it offers a way of understanding the limits of growth and how to share resources. It is here that business can draw inspiration from nature's principles.

Biomimicry is the practice of learning how the natural world designs itself, and applying that knowledge to how we farm, produce energy, manufacture products, heal ourselves and build things. In her book *Biomimicry: Innovation Inspired by Nature*, the natural sciences writer Janine Benyus describes nature's principles: nature runs on sunlight, uses only the energy it needs, fits form to function, recycles everything, rewards co-operation, banks diversity, demands local expertise, curbs excesses and taps the power of limits. These principles point us towards a productive way of thinking about business, as a philosophy and a practice. In doing so, they form the basis of questions about how a business could operate, and enable a reimagining and resetting of the benchmark of what it means to be in business.

Forward-facing companies use principles of biomimicry in their design, engineering, supply chains and business models. Consider the flooring manufacturer Interface, which set itself a goal to transform its business model to become climate-positive by working on carbon-negative products. This was a long journey, but its story is important as it shows that even an established company can embark on transformation.

Geanne van Arkel, the Head of Sustainable Development at EMEA (Europe, Middle East and Africa) Interface, says, 'We have no choice if we want to be in business in the medium and long term. We have raised the bar, and our goal now is to become a company that is regenerative. This is what everyone should want, otherwise there is no beauty in the things you do — be it living, working or doing business.'

As another example, look at Bolt Threads, which produces two innovative materials using production processes inspired by nature: Microsilk, inspired by the properties of spider silk, and Mylo, a leather material made from mycelium, part of a fungus. The manufacturing of textiles is the second-largest source of pollution on the planet. Bolt's materials are produced with less waste and fewer natural resources to reduce this environmental impact. Bolt envisions a world where we don't have to deplete or pollute our forests, oceans and rivers to benefit from their natural secrets. What if better days for our planet lie ahead?

Design

Design is not incidental to modern economies — it is integral. Everything man-made has been designed: culture, products, services, code, farming, architecture, materials, the chair you are sitting on and the backlit screen on your desk. Design opens up new ways of thinking about our environment. Good design always starts with a beautiful question: how can we use design to make the world a better place? How can we design better solutions? How do we design and build cities to be better places to live in?

The built environment shapes our lives in so many ways. The business of building needs careful attention and thought, because our entire world is made of structures. Architecture in its broadest sense is one of the most powerful devices for beauty, because it shapes not only individual lives, but societies as a whole. What we design and build should be invested with beauty and all that entails. Take a look at the working practice of the architect Alison Brooks, who believes that architecture should reclaim the language of beauty for buildings.

A RIBA award-winner, Brooks is often described as a leading architect of her generation. She is known for her urban regeneration projects, her elegant modernist buildings and her 'forward-thinking' civic masterplans. Brooks is an advocate of returning the language of beauty to the practice of architecture and urban design. She uses beauty as one of four foundations, along with authenticity, generosity and civicness, in a framework for creating the architecture we need today. Brooks's work can be found in the Accordia masterplan in Cambridge, as well as projects in Albert Crescent, Bath; South Kilburn, London; and the University of Northampton.

Brooks explains that modernism has a lot to answer for. In her view, beauty was excluded from what is described as the modern project of the city because of its negative association with the 19th-century City Beautiful movement. Now, we are returning our gaze to the legacy of urban parks, avenues and extraordinary civic buildings, still doing their intended job of elevating the human spirit. According to Brooks, they 'form a robust infrastructure for our 21st-century urban life through their generosity, civic idealism and craftsmanship'. This creates a more open world, encouraging communities to take root and to feel they have ownership of the public realm, where people can live harmoniously.

So, what could be the benefits of such an approach? Copenhagen looks set to become the world's first carbon-neutral city by 2025, with 100 new wind turbines. The Danish capital is setting a benchmark for green cities, with the aim of a 20 per cent reduction in heat and commercial electricity consumption; 75 per cent of all journeys to be made by bike, on foot or by public transport; becoming a world leader in converting organic waste into biogas; 60,000 square metres of new solar panels; and 100 per cent of the city's heating requirements to be met by renewables. And that's a beautiful thing.

Cities can be designers of better futures, too. The city of Amsterdam has committed itself to rethinking and redesigning how a city can become regenerative, how it can become a place that fosters an improved quality of life, founded on a long-term vision and a policy not to make exponential growth its purpose. These two liveable cities signpost how business can regenerate the environment.

Values and metrics

There is an ethical dimension to building a beautiful business. There is nothing wrong with making a profit, but you have to ask yourself: Why are you in business? Successful companies are increasingly defined by their values-based worldviews. These are mission-driven firms that strive for more compassionate, responsible and ecologically restorative ways of doing business in our world. Look at the trainer brand Veja, which believes that to build a future worth living in, we must try to achieve equilibrium between our economy, our ecology and our community. Consider the outdoor clothing manufacturer Patagonia, which is in the business of saving our planet.

Companies such as Veja and Patagonia are more attractive to talent, and become more effective in their leadership, because they are led by values. As I have said before, no one is perfect. Whatever we make, we are taking resources from somewhere, consuming energy, creating waste and using human labour. Yet by applying regenerative values and metrics, we can build a new framework, informing purpose, decision-making and definitions of success.

If this is the case, what are the values and metrics that a regenerative business should be using?

The values and metrics of a regenerative economy

Make no mistake, our world is deeply wounded, spiritually, ecologically and materially. And yes, we have done it to ourselves. Why? Because we have developed a set of rules based on a belief about what success as a civilisation looks like. Which is why now is the time to rewrite the constitutional rules of value. What do those values signify? How do we define the criteria for successful outcomes and how do we measure them?

	Extraction economy	Regenerative economy
Value creation metrics	**Takings**	**Contributions**
Main stakeholder	**Shareholder interest**	**Societal interest**
Success parameter	**Financial valuation**	**Social impact**
Growth paradigm	**Exponential**	**Circular**
Perspective / Life cycle	**Short term**	**Long term**
Workforce	**Human resource**	**Resourceful humans**
Divisions of labour	**Departments**	**Communities**
Leadership	**Command and control**	**Inspire and motivate**
Organisation	**Structure**	**Culture**

Value creation metrics of a regenerative economy. Alan Moore & Mads Thimmer

I have developed a set of value creation metrics for businesses operating in a regenerative economy. All businesses invested in regeneration can use these values and metrics to redesign themselves. Look at this table and use these metrics as an invitation to ask questions about how we can each contribute. How do we reconnect society? How can businesses create benefits for society and the environment that will also restore the economy?

Let's look at each of these areas in more depth.

1. Value creation metrics of a regenerative economy

Value creation metrics enable you to measure contributions. This links to the need of the end user. Consider what the world needs to heal and recover its equilibrium to thrive. How can your business contribute to this transformation? Beautiful businesses generate real value through creation, not the manipulation of markets or the non-returnable extraction of resources, either human or ecological.

2. Main stakeholder

Business is part of our society. Regard society as your main stakeholder, not shareholders. We are in service to the wider world. Our work reconnects society.

3. Success parameter

As we strive to do good in business, social and environmental impact becomes a success parameter. We seek social and environmental benefits, which are restorative to the planet and its people.

4. Growth paradigm

At a time of scarce resources, we seek a circular approach to growth, rather than pursuing exponential growth.

Progressive companies use materials for manufacturing that can be recycled or upcycled. They derive energy from renewable resources. They minimise extractive practices. They measure growth in the quality of life created.

5. Perspective / Life cycle

Take a long-term perspective: stop working in quarters and thinking in five-year plans. This will help to create a more restorative approach to plans. Think in generations to create legacy. Business then becomes a good ancestor.

6. Workforce

We must value each and every human being, and show respect for people's sovereignty and dignity. We are all entitled to the same rights. We need resourceful human beings, whole human beings and joyful human beings.

7. Divisions of labour

Community is everything. Look at new forms of collaboration — it's like a superpower. In a collaborative culture, communities are built on love, trust and transparency. They possess the ability to share decision-making throughout the community, bringing higher levels of effectiveness and efficiency.

8. Leadership

Consider the qualities of leadership for a progressive business as being inspirational, creative, empathetic, compassionate and inclusive. This is leadership that is rooted not in power and authority; its strength lies in transformative service and wisdom.

The organisation has a rich, vibrant culture and a non-hierarchical structure. Its governance and beliefs are steeped in values with a purpose of bettering the planet and restoring society. Organisations must create belonging beyond the financial transaction of the monthly pay cheque. A sense of belonging is nurtured through the cultures we create from the stories we tell and the values we share. This is where the best work is done. These organisations are more adaptive to the complex, fluid world in which we live.

Governance

This regenerative economy is gathering pace. Across the world, businesses are waking up to the benefits of becoming what is known as a B Corp. Certified B Corporations are businesses that meet the highest standards of verified social and environmental performance, public transparency and legal accountability to balance profit and purpose. This serves as a clear statement of purpose in working towards reduced inequality, lower levels of poverty, a healthier environment, stronger communities and the creation of more high-quality jobs with dignity.

High-profile members of B Corp include the outdoor clothing manufacturer Patagonia, the trainer brand Veja and the ethical bank Triodos. B Corporations are accelerating a shift in global culture to redefine success in business and to build a more inclusive and sustainable economy.

This is the statement of intention of certified B Corps:

— That we must be the change we seek in the world.

— That all business ought to be conducted as if people and place mattered.

— That, through their products, practices and profits, businesses should aspire to do no harm and benefit all.

— To do so requires that we act with the understanding that we are each dependent upon one another and thus responsible for each other and future generations.

When a business becomes a B Corp, it doesn't just join, pay a fee and wave a badge. There is a certification and verification programme, introducing legal requirements to consider the wider impact of their decisions, which is repeated every three years. The B Corp assessment measures performance across five areas: governance, workers, community, environment and customers. By going through this certification process, a company can increase its capability to build a business the world needs.

If you are running a progressive business, it is critical to get your governance right. One practical step is to plug into a legal framework and a company structure that is built on the need to move beyond the current model of business, predicated on exponential growth and all that means. In taking this step, whether you are a small business or a large company, starting up or on your way, you become part of the new ecology of business. And that's a really good thing.

3
**Generous
leadership**

If you are a leader, you are a builder. And if you are building something, make sure you build well. Here, I offer reflections on how to become a beautiful leader by instilling certain kinds of values, a positive mindset and good working practices.

Being a good ancestor

Some of us have got used to the idea of the winner takes it all, with no need to give back or pay things forward. That attitude has many consequences, none of which seem good. It does not matter whether you are a business of one or building something bigger.

The questions you must ask are: What am I leaving for others? Am I being a good ancestor?

This will help you to make difficult decisions, frame your path and re-evaluate what wealth and success look like. It is a sanity check that you can take on a daily, weekly, monthly or yearly basis. As the philosopher and novelist Iris Murdoch wrote in *The Sovereignty of Good*, 'the concept "good" is not the name of an esoteric object, it is the tool of every rational man'.

What world do you want to make?

What gets you out of bed on a Monday morning when it is pouring with rain? When it hurts like hell, what keeps you going? What is the deep well you draw from that fuels your best creativity? 'World-making' is the reason, the fire that stokes the furnace. This is the north star on the path that takes you home to your true self, serving as a beacon to others. It is about being true to yourself. It's not about money or reward, nor is it a theoretical exercise. Companies that care about the world they make create bonds and relationships with people who share those values and worldviews.

The coffee buyer Falcon Coffees wishes 'to change the way coffee is traded for good'. This is no mean feat, as coffee is traded as a commodity. As a result, the 26 million people who make it their business to grow the world's coffee, meeting people's insatiable thirst for the stuff, are also often treated as commodities. Falcon Coffees challenges that exploitative way of working by building supply chains with rural farming communities for mutual profit and positive social impact.

The Japanese martial artist Morihei Ueshiba, who created Aikido in the early twentieth century, did so with the aim of protecting all life that exists on this planet. The computer mouse inventor Doug Engelbart, who pioneered hypertext and video conferencing, wanted to help people to share knowledge, so they could collectively solve some of the world's most pressing problems. As a founder, consider your business's mission. Ask yourself, what world do you want to make? How do you wish to live?

The practice of a leader

Your first responsibility is to yourself. Are you in good shape mentally, spiritually and physically? How you move through the world is based on the quality of your being. Set aside time for your practice every day. Doing work on oneself is a good preparation for bringing one's best self into this world. It is the quality of your thoughts and the quality of your actions that bring love, compassion, wisdom and the right action into this world.

Michelin-starred chef Christian Puglisi of Relae in Denmark spoke to me about the beauty in the daily practice of helping his staff to become precise cooks, working on the menu, improving the experience of his customers — and himself. The action of progressing with the greatest passion and the greatest energy is a lifetime's work. See yourself as a work in progress.

Generosity as leadership

Generosity and business do not always go hand-in-hand. However, Guido Bernardinelli, CEO of La Marzocco, founded in 1927 and still privately owned, has spoken of its merits. When asked how his company has managed to survive, thrive and innovate, he has simply replied: 'total devotion to our people'. La Marzocco builds some of the best handmade espresso coffee machines in the world.

Approaching leadership with a sense of generosity taps into the greatest human qualities. In business, as in life, you should always strive to give back more than you take. Generosity is nurturing for people. Creating the right conditions for your staff to thrive is key to being the best and most effective leader that you can be.

The Icelandic artist Olafur Eliasson opened my eyes to the possibility of generosity, by feeding around a hundred of his staff every day with a freshly cooked vegetarian meal. Eliasson says, 'Cooking is caring for others. It is a gesture of generosity.' He states that eating together brings a connection between human beings, food and the sun. Generosity begins with an invitation, and in capable hands brings a rich flow of information, so a deeper understanding of the world evolves. Eliasson has teams with specific functions, working on a range of projects. He wants them to feel that they are interwoven; he does so by showing he truly cares. As the South Korean Buddhist nun and cook Jeong Kwan says, with food what we are really eating is the 'mindset of sharing'. This is generosity. In your own work, consider asking the question: How can you show generosity as a leader in a way that will feed the cultural fabric of your business?

The empathetic leader

We judge. We judge ourselves. We judge others. Judgement affects behaviour and the actions we then take. On my life's journey, I have been, at times, a terrible judge of myself, which has taken me into some dark places, as well as being a harsh judge of others; in so doing, I've behaved in ways that I regret. Through my journey, I've realised there is personal work to do. What I have learned is that empathy is like a superpower. Overleaf is a true story about empathy and leadership.

Tashi and the Monk

The Buddhist monk Lobsang was trained under the guidance of His Holiness the Dalai Lama, but some years ago he left behind a life as a spiritual teacher in the United States to build a community in the foothills of the Himalayas. There, he looks after orphaned and neglected children. Five-year-old Tashi is the newest arrival. Her mother has recently died and she has been abandoned by her alcoholic father.

Tashi is wild, disruptive and aggressive towards other children. There are tears: Tashi is deeply troubled as she has been deeply wounded. As the University of Houston professor Brené Brown, an authority on vulnerability and leadership, writes: 'pain that is not transformed is transmitted'. Tashi is in full transmission mode. There is a moment when the teacher finds it too much. And there is too much disruption for the children around Tashi. She has to go and see Monk Lobsang.

They sit down together. Lobsang could do a number of things: he could shout, punish or even expel Tashi. What he does instead is to listen and talk with this young, angry girl with great compassion and empathy. It is a turning point for Tashi, as she has never known love, compassion or tenderness. All she knows is how to punch the world and those who are in it. Fear, judgement, rejection and being abandoned are powerful drivers of destructive human behaviour because they are blueprints that say we are not enough. If the feeling of not being enough is the source of our behaviour, we cannot connect to our true potential. How many of us are like that?

Monk Lobsang's act of empathy is a gift for Tashi, which means she can begin to walk for the first time on a healthier path. The importance of making a human connection is seen in the words of Brené Brown: 'Empathy has no script. There is no right way or wrong way to do it. It's simply listening, holding space, withholding judgment, emotionally connecting, and communicating that incredibly healing message of "You're not alone".'

By receiving empathy, not only do we understand how good it feels to be heard and accepted, we can also better understand the courage that it takes to share that need for empathy in the first place. Tashi's story speaks to me because I know that the root of anger is fear. I also know what it means to be tested. Today, I follow a mantra: 'No matter what the provocation, it is never wise to respond in anger.' Anger saps authority.

A leader's ability to be truly empathetic shows strength, not vulnerability. This is a nurturing quality. It allows one to see far deeper into the truth of people and to find their potential. If you show empathy, people will then reveal their potential to you. This courageous act means you have empowered and strengthened your organisation and its potential. Empathy is an investment that will repay you.

How to apply empathy in the workplace

Imagine you are running a team that could be described as having high expectations for the delivery of an innovative product or service. There is a desired outcome, but the pathway is unknown. Many challenges are encountered and feedback is necessary, from talking on a one-to-one basis to collaboration with the team.

Consider whether there could be simple rules: of listening deeply, never interrupting and offering constructive input.

While no one is told what to do, suggestions are made. Since things have not worked out as desired, let's see them as learning opportunities. The framing and language are key to how we respond and engage. We create our best work in a space marked by love, not fear.

Questions that an empathetic leader asks

— What would be the behaviour and language that will bring out the best in your team?

— Can you define a set of guidelines for empathetic leadership?

— Is there a means to welcome new recruits on board through empathetic practice?

— Is there a way that you can mentor and walk with team members, helping them grow into their full potential?

Ethical decision-making

There is no shortcut to creating worthwhile outcomes. I have seen too many decisions made for short-term gain, where constant growth in the service of profit becomes a sickness, which can be terminal. Look at a situation when you feel deadlines pressing so hard there is no time or air to breathe. How do you as a leader deal with intense pressure, managing the expectations of investors, board members and those within the team?

Imagine a company at a board meeting. The firm is under pressure. Decisions must be made to counter its ailing financial performance. A number of board members have come up with a ruse to fabricate evidence, enabling the company to sell its products falsely. It's a risky plan because if the deception were to be discovered, the consequences could be disastrous: a fall in market valuation; a loss of trust in the brand, which would impact sales; fatal damage to the leadership team; and the high costs of legal action. This could be the legacy of making such a choice.

But what if someone asks a question: 'Is that the most ethical decision we can make?'

It's a simple question, but is packed with important frames for business decision-making: how to stand in truth, how to be guided instinctively to a better outcome, how to discover a path based on values, and how to retain the concept of legacy building. If you are a disruptive leader, this question encourages you to resist the urge to break things, and instead use the time to build. There is a saying that what happens in vagueness stays in vagueness. This question helps to illuminate an ambiguous world and to navigate to a better destination.

Beautiful decision-making

To build a business the world needs, we have to be prepared to create products or services that are both beautiful and profitable. The question, 'Is that the most beautiful decision we can make?' asks you to be fully open with your mindset and to embrace challenges with optimism. I use this question when working with organisations. In group settings, I have witnessed how the question calls for people to give truthful answers. Here are some examples of useful follow-up questions:

— How does this affect me?

— How does this affect my organisation?

— What was I not seeing before?

— How does this affect the culture of the company?

— How does this change my thoughts about my leadership capability?

— Are there transformational opportunities, which previously were unseen?

— How could our organisation create and deliver greater value?

— How could we radically redesign the business?

The fundamental 'beautiful decision' question steers the imagination to find an alternative path, informing the right action. It provides and asks for crystal-clear clarity. As we shall see in the next chapter, focusing on the carpet tile manufacturer, Interface, it may be a tough question to answer. But then no one said it would be easy. I would rather be known as a profitable pioneer with a future ahead of me, than dumped on the scrapheap of failed businesses because we rushed to claim a false prize. You are never too big to fail.

Consider asking, 'Is that the most beautiful decision we can make?' within your own organisation. It does not have to be for a matter of high strategic importance. It could be about an everyday issue. Reflect on a situation that has happened or one that is upcoming, where decisions made will shape your future. This simple question reframes what a good outcome could be. Those who ask a more beautiful question could find a more beautiful answer.

4
**Your
company
culture**

Culture is the foundation of any organisation, the unique psychological coding that shapes how we engage and interact with each other, how we speak, what we talk about, how we are made to feel, and how we make decisions. It's important because culture decides what gets done. I believe work-based cultures premised upon empathy, generosity and reciprocity can release the full creative potential of an organisation, allowing it to take on new challenges with optimism. They allow high performance teams to work without fear in an environment where adaptiveness and innovation flow. And who wouldn't want that?

Change your mind to change the world

You may have already built a successful business. But what if your values have changed? What if you see a world that could be better if you were to redesign what you do and how you do it? Even an established company can change its mind.

The global carpet tile manufacturer Interface was founded by Ray C. Anderson and incorporated as a company in 1973. The organisation pioneered the idea of tessellating carpet tiles, meeting the need of an economy that fell in love with the idea of 'big': a big economy, big companies, big offices and big financial returns. Think *Dallas* and the Southfork Ranch in Texas. By 1978, Interface sales had reached $11 million. The company went public in 1983. It now has a market cap of $1.53 billion.

In its early years, Interface was not a good friend to the environment: its extraction of natural resources and the processes of manufacturing contributed to high levels of CO_2, causing pollution and creating products that inevitably ended up in landfill. Then Anderson had an epiphany, thanks to reading the entrepreneur Paul Hawken's *The Ecology of Commerce*, notably the chapter 'The Death of Birth' on the loss of biodiversity.

The founder decided that things had to change. Anderson went to his institutional investors and shared his vision of a company that would be fully sustainable by 2020. The response was, 'Great, Ray, but can it make more money than the current business?' Determined to show them that it could, Anderson initiated Mission Zero. Sadly, Ray Anderson died in 2011. But his world-making vision has thrived.

Today, Interface's Net-Works programme enables fishing communities in developing countries to give discarded fishing nets a second life by selling them back into the global supply chain, providing a source of recycled materials for use in carpet tile production. In so doing, the company has built an inclusive circular business model. But recycled and upcycled materials are not only coming through the Net-Works programme.

Interface's mission is to source and develop, together with its suppliers, 100 per cent recycled and bio-based materials for its flooring production. With its new initiative Climate Takeback, the company is innovating the development of carbon-negative products, such as its

Proof Positive tile capturing 2kg of carbon in one square metre of carpet tile, and its CircuitBac Green carpet-backing product.

This is a story of large-scale organisational change, which involves the redesign and the re-engineering of a business model and supply chain. An organisation has decided to operate on a new set of values and principles. This is a narrative of 'beautiful unreason': a company and its environmentally and socially harmful short-term demand for profit challenges business orthodoxy.

Doing good is good for business. Think about your own company culture as you read through this set of ideas.

1. Shoot for the moon

The more ambitious and aspirational your mission, the greater its power. Be unreasonable. Don't settle for incremental goals. If you want to transform something, set a goal that you don't know how to achieve yet.

2. A change in mindset can change everything

Embracing the need for change with your heart and mind is essential. From the outset, be open and willing to see that there is always the possibility for a different approach and a better way of doing things.

3. Every vision needs a plan

To make a vision a reality, you need a mission, a plan, and a way to measure success. It's impossible to reach a breakthrough ambition if you don't have a credible action plan.

4. Take a circular approach

You can make progress by building a circular system, but this only goes so far on its own. To change your entire system, you have to engage your whole supply chain — meaning all those who are engaged with the business, in one way or another — to create a truly circular model.

5. To change everything, you need everyone
It's one thing to have a mission, but making progress means getting every single one of your people connected. This means inspiring everyone to feel personally invested in playing their part.

6. A wrong turn can lead to the right result
It is never a linear process. Embrace failures as necessary steps on the path to progress. Every pioneer in history has had to stay the course, learn from mistakes and keep going when things go wrong, as they often will.

7. Be transparent
Be so transparent that it feels uncomfortable. Tell the full story and share 'whole company metrics'. Pilot and push new approaches to disclosure and transparency that can be scaled to your industry and beyond.

8. Start a ripple to create a wave
To have a real impact on the world, you need to influence others to follow your lead and help them to lead the way for others. That's how a ripple effect can take on a life of its own, increasing positive impacts to a scale well beyond what you could achieve alone.

9. Raise the bar
Know when you need a new challenge, or when you need to change the target. Challenge yourself to embrace a transformational next step. Create the processes and dialogues internally and externally to help you see the future.

Build a learning environment

I have worked as a craftsman all my life. Initially, I was a designer of books and catalogues, working alongside visual artists such as Anselm Kiefer, Richard Long, Cecil Collins and Helen Chadwick. I have always believed in the idea that my work serves a wider social purpose. The practice of craftsmanship has never deserted me.

Since moving into business, I've worked on long-term assignments with teams, where my first task has often been to create a learning environment, to support my team with upgrading their skills, to bring them closer together and to improve collaboration and personal development.

I initiated this process with the intention that we would then do better work, make work more meaningful, and incline people to a higher aspiration to create products and services of greater value and quality. It was second nature to me to do so. I modelled this approach on a craft-based workshop.

The best workplace environments are social spaces, premised on the idea and practice of the craft workshop that inculcates an environment built on trust, openness, diversity, exploration, practice and knowledge that is held, developed and shared. This creates a space for reflection, and for personal and professional development. It also builds a deeper sense of connection and community. Work that becomes meaningful is a characteristic associated with craftsmanship.

Years later, I came across the sociologist Richard Sennett's book *The Craftsman*, which offers an exploration into the practice of craftsmanship. Sennett showed how the practice could be at the epicentre of social good in modern society. His view is that craftsmanship is an innate capability in all of us, and that 'nature furnished humanity at large with the intelligence to do good work (craft skills)'.

It is this knowledge of the deep social constructs of craftsmanship that allows us to envision how, as individuals and human beings, we can re-engage meaningfully with the world, work and each other. All craftwork is in one way or another 'being in service to others', and that is what makes it different as a frame for life.

Craft connects the dignity of work with the idea that you can be doing, learning and growing more. Businesses need to bring the culture of craft, as a way of working, into their organisations. The tools of craft can help to build a company's culture.

5
**Products
and services:
13 design
questions**

What you bring into this world is up to you. I don't know what the future holds. But what I do know is that even the minutest detail of good design can touch all our lives — and good design is central to what we bring into our world.

We can use design to buoy the human spirit, to uplift us physically and spiritually, connecting us to our human nature. Design elevates, nurtures and improves our lot. It intertwines our spiritual and material wellbeing. I am always seeking new ways to interpret that belief and philosophy.

The early to mid-twentieth-century pioneers of design and architecture embraced the idea of transforming society to create a better world. In Germany, the multi-disciplinary Bauhaus school, founded by Paul Klee, Wassily Kandinsky, Walter Gropius and Mies van der Rohe, became the beacon that would ignite a broader movement towards social and economic transformation. Yet this is not the only place where we find architects, designers, artists and craftspeople working towards the manifestation of a better world. Finnish architects Alvar and Aino Aalto, Danish designers Arne Jacobsen and Verner Panton, and Finnish designer Eero Arnio all embodied the same ideals as their central European cousins, and all drew from the visionary work of John Ruskin and William Morris.

What follows are 13 questions that every founder should ask in order to fill our world with optimism.

Does it matter?

We start with a series of questions: Does it matter? Does it matter to you? Does it matter to your team or the company? More importantly, how does it matter to the world? What we, as pioneers of innovation, bring into this world should constantly be questioned.

People assume that innovation is automatically a good thing; I believe innovation should exist to make people's lives better. Too often innovation is used as an excuse to extract more money from people, without improving their lives. This is where 'The Mattering' is relevant — it gives a sense of the difference one makes in the world. It connects to the aspiration for social and economic transformation: business in service to society and to the earth. It *matters* that we honour both. It is foundational to the restoration of the equilibrium between economy, ecology and society. It matters that we are making a positive contribution in this regenerative economy. It matters that we plan and act for the long term.

The industrial designer Dieter Rams considers that good design is innovative, useful and long-lasting. He says, 'The time of thoughtless design for thoughtless consumption is over.' You climb the highest mountains when everyone understands why it matters.

Is it transformative?

As a maker, you must bring things into this world that are meaningful, valuable and useful, things that say, 'Life can be better.' How are you making lives better? How are you nurturing your workplace and workforce? How are you creating an environment where all can thrive in your municipality? How are you taking an entire industry and transforming it for the better? This could mean eradicating waste and bad practice, having the vision to see new ideas, and having the courage and the conviction to seek and implement lasting beneficial change. If it's not transformative as a business, then you are not in business.

Is it regenerative?

This is a key question because the language of sustainability is limiting us. Sustainability has become an overused and diluted word, and it has been treated as a destination. You can go through a checklist and tick enough boxes, and then you are a sustainable business. Climate change fills us with dread, but is a state of dread where you want to live in your heart and mind? Regeneration must live in the everyday world. Regeneration offers us a means to redesign how we live and how we work. It is filled with the language of nurture, wellbeing, joy and hope. Universally, we all want these things.

The simple principle is: you give back more than you take. In the process of making, growing, working, educating, all human activity must be premised on regeneration. Paul Hawken argues that what we need are solutions that regenerate human, ecological and economic wellbeing. 'They're the same thing,' he says. 'Regenerating atmosphere is what happens when you regenerate a village, a fishery, a forest, a farm, a city, a transport system and the ocean. They're all interconnected.'

Your supply chain needs to become one that is not extractive and refuses to treat anything or anyone as a commodity. You are not being anywhere near as efficient or productive as you could be, if you continue to work on an extractive model of business. In the things we create, we equally need to bring in beauty, compassion and empathy, whether thinking about policies, workplace cultures, or even how we farm our land.

Coding beauty

How can this be applied to the digital realm? Can you code beauty? We fret about artificial intelligence (AI) and the impact of the growth of automation. Yet what if the coding of AI were directed by the concept of beauty? One possibility that I find attractive is the view of Stanford University professor Fei-Fei Li, who says: 'I often tell my students not to be misled by the name "artificial intelligence" — there is nothing artificial about it. AI is made by humans, intended to behave like humans, and, ultimately, to impact human lives and human society.' It is the intention with which we pick up a tool that shapes what we make.

One challenge with AI is that the codes themselves, the algorithms, can build themselves and transmute into new things, which you may not have envisaged. However, that can be turned to our advantage, if we can develop self-learning code, which constantly builds itself, defends itself and transposes itself into something even more useful. Now, that sounds positive. It could even be beautiful. How about an AI algorithm that is constantly improving itself to work on behalf of humanity?

Building for life

Then we come to businesses that create products using materials that derive from the finite resources of the earth. Consider two UK-based companies, Vitsoe and Naim.

The first produces shelving for the home, the second makes home sound equipment. Both design their products to last for a very long time. If you have to take something and can't give it back, then respect its origins and keep it for life.

The only business model you will ever need

'The Total' is a term created by Gabriel Branby, the founder of a company that makes axes, Gransfors Bruk. Holistic in its concept, the term is an economic way of looking at our world, based around what we take, make and waste. All businesses are faced with costs associated with all three. 'The Total' encompasses ethics, business, production process, products and the world that we inhabit. Branby says we have an unlimited responsibility for 'The Total', a responsibility that we try but do not always succeed in fulfilling. Reframing a business to operate along this model increases efficiency and effectiveness, and also improves financial resilience. This is not a new concept. It was the basis upon which all indigenous tribes around the world operated. We have thrown a great deal of wisdom away in the name of progress.

If you are not working towards zero carbon and zero waste; if you are not using circular manufacturing processes; if you are not working with design and production methodologies inspired by nature; then your business model is out of date and out of time. Increasingly, over the next 25 years we are likely to see legislation that penalises wasteful and harmful production methodologies and the use of fossil-based production technologies and businesses. As the outgoing head of the Bank of England Mark Carney observed, just before he left his post, those institutions continuing to 'invest in fossil fuels' will realise in the very near future that these will all become worthless assets.

Today, as I write while the rain beats unrelentingly on my windows, Australia is burning. 'The Total' originates from nature's business model. Nature uses everything. Her law is that you do not consume everything. If that happens, the show rolls the final film credits: that's all, folks.

Is it useful?

Everything has utility. A spoon has utility, though I have met some spoons that were not terribly useful. The role of a product, a service, a spoon or a car park should be about enhancing people's lives or increasing our productivity. The things we make should be restorative and solve seemingly intractable problems. They should elevate our everyday lives in getting stuff done.

Utility should also have elegance and be infused with grace. There is a choreography of use, which is how we can frame the objects and tools we use — the interplay between the object, the user and the space, which is where we can create beauty and elevate utility into something life-enhancing. Throughout our entire lives, we are constantly in a state of choreography with tools and objects.

Usefulness is not an excuse for poor work, or for using the wrong materials. Confining beauty to visual appreciation and excluding beauty from practical objects has turned out to be a grave error of modern man.

There was a moment in the twentieth century when industrial designers, architects and civic planners were all engaged with the idea that design was part of a social revolution. They saw their work as world-making, liberating and improving people's lives for the better in the everyday.

Danish furniture designers, whose work was mass-produced, retained the essence of the materials' origin, and the love of a human hand in its making. The Finnish architects Alvar and Aino Aalto believed that architects should conceive of their buildings as *'Gesamtkunstwerke'* or total works of art, including not just the structure and its shape. Everything should be considered and designed. The Aaltos imbued their work with great utility, innovation and humanity.

Consider applying those principles and ideas to an unusual context. Accountancy, one could argue, has a sense of utility. Small and medium-sized enterprises (SMES) are big employers. Accountancy is necessary, but the professional services provided are vast in their spectrum of quality. There are consequences when accountants do not deliver a high level of service. Accountancy, you could say, is not a beautiful business to be in.

Yet accountancy can be well designed in terms of utility and experience. Xero is a software accountancy platform that serves SMES. It answers the question, 'Why do I spend so much time on accounting?' Elegant, simple and intuitive, Xero also uses automation to deliver a high-quality service to its customers, globally. Nothing like Xero existed before Xero. In 2019, its market cap exceeded £8 billion. Xero has demonstrated just how beautiful the day-to-day utility of accountancy can be. This is reminiscent of the practice of the great Japanese craftsman Soetsu Yanagi, who held the belief that a profound knowledge of beauty can be acquired by seeking it in utilitarian objects, rooted in daily life.

Can you create a joyful experience?

I can remember learning to ride my first bicycle; it was red. As a memory, the sheer joy of being able to balance and power myself forward into the world has never left me. Years later, I had the added joy of motorcycling up the highest mountain on a Greek island with a good friend. To stand in a pine-scented forest, looking down at the bay where I swam, early morning, in crystal-clear waters as small fishing boats slumbered was another moment of sensual revelation. Holding my first iPhone* as my fingers swiped, rotated, tapped an intuitive screen, was a moment of sensual epiphany. I still use my old iPod because its navigation wheel designed for the human thumb still gives me joy, yes, joy. Designed by Jony Ive, it represents how design can be transformative, even in the smallest of ways. All design is sensual.

I feel joy when the landscape is flooded with winter sun, slung low in the sky, the air clean with optimism. Similarly, I have watched the smiling faces of people using a fully automated multi-storey car park in Åarhus in Denmark. I use them all as guides to how I want to use design. Everything is experience, good and bad.

---

* All our mobile devices contain finite rare-earth elements. They quietly tell us that our world is finite too.

Joy has to be core to your design work: real, memorable joy. As a designer, I want to know: What does this experience feel like? How do we create joyful experiences? How will it feel otherworldly? How will it fill us with wonder? What senses do we wish to engage? Where can we look for inspiration? The joy of the mountain peak, the smell of baking bread or an idea that takes us into details, such as 'Ma'.

Ma shows that the special appeal of Japanese music lies almost completely in its rhythms, which involve delicate variations and delays between notes, known as *Ma* (spaces). To the Japanese, *Ma* are everything. *Ma* takes its inspiration from nature. A Kabuki actor, talking to the author Alex Kerr, explains, 'Have you ever been in the mountains and listened to the cuckoo? It says *cuckoo, cuckoo*, with the slightest pause between syllables. It doesn't say *kuku-kuku* like a metronome.'

Is what you create elegant?

My mentor, the designer Derek Birdsall, would often say, 'Alan, you should always make your work elegant.' His sideways glance, hand gesture and the impeccable deep tone of his voice stated the obvious. As a younger man, I struggled with his invitation, his challenge to me, to make everything elegant, as we talked about design, typography and related things. As I grew, I could see elegance in Derek's craft, in his work. I also thought about my father. He was born in 1929 in Haggerston, one of the roughest areas of east London, but was always elegant in a humble way. We have a choice.

I took this as a principle, a pathway to test my work as to its elegance and usefulness. When you unpack elegance as an idea, it possesses many applications in creating beautiful businesses. Is your company's workplace culture elegant? Do the products and services that you and your company design feel elegant? Is the user experience elegant? How do you serve your customers?

Elegance for me is about discovering beauty living in everyday things. It can be invisible, like a thread woven with such skill that it makes all the difference, but you would never know to look at it. Elegance is part of a mindset; it's a philosophy, a behaviour and a design principle.

Are you making a thing of quality?

The quality of thought, in turn, manifests in the quality of action. Even how we move through life is nothing more than the quality of our being. Quality is where all good materials come from, how they are grown. Quality is how we work, the conditions in which we work. Quality is the experience we create for others. Quality can be seen in ingredients and their provenance, the experience created and how they are served. Quality asks us to be our very best — the best that we can be. That requires discipline. The idea of quality asks for consistency and a standard to be set.

Time plays an important role, because works of quality take time to build. Look at the Japanese construction company Kongō Gumi, founded back in 578, which was the world's oldest continuously operating independent company, hand-building Buddhist temples until 2006, when it became a subsidiary of a larger company. *Takumi* is the Japanese term for a 'master craftsman', who has put in many thousands of hours to perfect a craft skill. Kongō Gumi employs *takumi* who design and make buildings of the very highest quality. This takes time, discipline, practice and focus. Works of quality tend to last.

Here are the principles the company runs on:

— Always use common sense

— Concentrate on your core business

— Ensure long-term stability for employees

— Maintain balance between work and family

— Listen to your customers and treat them with respect

— Always submit the cheapest and most honest estimates

— Drink only in moderation

How will the language we use define us?

All culture starts with language. Language is meaning-making; it frames and holds worldviews. Look at our current world and see how leaders and politicians use language to frame mindsets and beliefs. This can have deeply divisive results.

I know through my work that the language we use can create a space, an environment and a culture that is collaborative, that holds and nurtures trust, and celebrates creativity and autonomy. This is all down to our choice of words. If we use the language of war, how does that affect us? If we use the language of power, this could influence actions taken. As the writer Toni Morrison said, 'Word-work is sublime ... because it is generative; it makes meaning that secures our difference, our human difference — the way in which we are like no other life.'

This application of language, what we say and how we express ourselves, becomes the nervous system of an organisation. It starts on the inside and manifests on the outside, defining how we act and what we believe in.

Will you use the language of empathy and compassion? Strip away the jargon. Use plain language with craft and skill. Even make your language poetic.

Is it truthful?

'Beauty is truth, truth, beauty,' wrote the poet John Keats in *Ode on a Grecian Urn*, concluding that that is 'all ye need to know'. Your business must feel truthful: true to its purpose, truthful as to how its supply chain works. Transparency is the sunshine in which truth flourishes. If we believe a person, a business or an organisation is being truthful, then we can have a dialogue that is very different from a shallow conversation. As the philosopher Onora O'Neill suggested, organisations should not try to be trusted; rather they should aim to demonstrate trustworthiness, which requires honesty, competence and reliability.

Your business model should feel honest. Businesses that obscure the buying process, making it needlessly opaque, lurk in the darkness. It is always better to stand in truth. There are a growing number of businesses, ranging from the industries of confectionery to transportation, with supply chains and business practices that show radical transparency. Plus, there is a growing demand for clear provenance and traceability in supply chains.

Ethics and simple honesty form the basis of good society. Let's face it: business is part of our society. So, it's integral to the working practice of conducting a business, that you have a set of honest standards.

Does it feel inevitable?

Imagine how good it feels to be sitting in the original Monmouth Coffee Shop in Covent Garden, founded in 1978. How does that chair feel as you sit to read this? How is this intuitive? What makes the transformational design piece feel so good that you are glad to be here?

Or how do you feel at home as you walk into a hotel? Experience is all about feeling and navigating through this world. Experiencing a sense of inevitability removes friction: it feels naturally good.

Any experience should feel inevitable. It's the moment when we surrender to wonder. Wonder is joyful. It means we are fully engaged, committed to the experience as it takes us inside a different world. I have used this principle for the things I have designed in my life. The natural world is full of wonder. I don't walk on the vast expanse of Holkham Beach in Norfolk where the land, sea and sky meet, experiencing all its majesty, and then want to redesign it. I am simply in a state of wonder and joy.

A great deal of work goes into designing inevitability. It is a form of seduction, as the experience is so complete that it means you are not resisting, but you have succumbed. Whenever you design or make anything, the one thing you must ask is, 'How will it feel inevitable so that people could not imagine it any other way?' When we have a really good experience, we do tend to want to come back for some more, as well as tell our friends. I have walked on Holkham Beach for the last 30 years. I drink my coffee when I can at Monmouth Coffee Shop on Monmouth Street in Covent Garden.

Would you want to sell these products and services to your family?

A while back, I was running a Beautiful Business design and leadership programme with the CEO plus 70 divisional heads of a large company. After a series of exercises, a woman stood up in front of the leadership group to make this statement: 'We should be making products and services we would want to sell to our families.'

There was a moment of silence. Applying beauty to business does interesting things to people. Perhaps the idea of only making things you would willingly sell to friends and family was not as obvious as I had first assumed. To this woman, it had become a question of social purpose. She realised her business was part of society, not separate from it. The company was interwoven with family, community, villages, towns and cities.

The question is, then, who are you serving? If you are not making products and services that your family would wish to use, what exactly are you doing?

Will you enjoy the process?

'Why does it matter?' is connected to the creative process and enjoyment. Creating enduring beauty or building a beautiful business can be, and often is, hard. It takes perseverance when you are facing pushback against challenging the business orthodoxy of the status quo. No one said it would be easy. Embrace the hardship and enjoy it, because you are alive and in the eye of the storm. This is when, having set your business right, you know whatever storm you are in, you will get through it and succeed. Enjoy the process.

How will you create legacy?

What are you going to leave behind for others? For society, for the earth? Your work could become contributory, deepening the potential of our world.

6
**Two case
studies**

Veja: how to design and build an ethical business

TWO CASE STUDIES

> We decided to make sneakers, because this product is a symbol for our generation and our era. It's also a product that crystallises the major issues of globalisation through its production, dissemination, and usage.
>
> ---
>
> Sébastien Kopp, co-founder of Veja

With its stylish offering crafted in Brazil, Veja takes its name from the Portuguese word for look, *'veja'*. In this case, let's look beyond the trainers and look at how they're made.

Trainer manufacturer Veja is a business that's really committed to regeneration, from how it sources raw materials in an ethical and sustainable fashion to how it processes and manufactures its products. Who the company employs, how it ships its goods, and even where it buys its electricity, all demonstrate the new desire of companies to be world-makers of businesses, putting their purpose before profit.

In founding the company, Sébastien Kopp and François-Ghislain Morillion were motivated by their personal experiences of unfair and unethical business practices. They witnessed the unsustainable practices of harvesting and processing raw materials, which cause catastrophic damage to humans and the environment. They asked themselves: Could they make a business another way, end-to-end? Could they build one where environmental justice and social justice were integral? They also believed that companies globally hold more power than politicians or even sovereign states. If we want to offer another model, Kopp argued, let's try to create a company from scratch that makes a difference. With a view to embarking on their journey of 'commercial disobedience', they established Veja in 2004 with a €50,000 loan.

Why did they select trainers, when they had no experience in the fashion industry? Because trainers spoke to their generation. But how to start? They asked a question few, it seems, do: How is our product actually made? The founders went back to the beginning of the supply chain. Where does the raw material come from? As they discovered answers to their questions, they moved forward to the next set of questions on how to replace the environmentally unfriendly raw materials with natural, eco-friendly ones. Which is how they arrived in Brazil, looking for sustainably harvested rubber, only to be found growing wild in the Amazon. It was time to learn Portuguese.

To these novice students of the trainer and its manufacturing processes, learning about organic cotton opened their minds to the scale of immediate damage, combined with the long-term harm, that growing non-organic cotton inflicts on the growers and their environment. In Brazil, the organic farmers Kopp and Morillion spoke to wanted to have nothing more to do with the chemical production of cotton, which made them mortally sick.

Veja now works with small producer co-operatives in Brazil in the growing of the cotton (organically), the harvesting of rubber and the assembly of its products.

The rubber comes from the Amazon, one of the few places where rubber trees grow wild. Veja buys the rubber at a premium, ensuring there is no commercial incentive to turn to logging or land clearance and so protecting the environment. The negotiation with *seringueiro* families (those who harvest and process the rubber) took several years for trust to be established. Leather used for the shoe collections is tanned with acacia extracts, a natural, non-polluting alternative to heavy metals, such as chrome. Unlike modern tanning processes, this reduces the risk of serious water pollution. The company tests for chemicals that could be harmful. Veja also manufactures vegan shoes.

Since 2004, Veja has set the price of its organic and agro-ecological cotton in advance, in agreement with the state of Ceará producer associations. Since the price is uncorrelated to the stock market and its fluctuations, the contracts are likely to offer the producers greater financial security than being linked to the stock-market cycle. This security is all the stronger since they know how much they are going to earn from the cotton before they even plant it. Veja also pays a €0.2 collective premium per kilo of cotton to the associations to improve working conditions.

In France, Veja works with Ateliers Sans Frontières, a French social charity, that promotes the professional integration of people who are excluded from the labour market, by offering them a suitable paid job, personalised social support and help to develop a career plan. They are responsible for receiving trainers shipped from Brazil, organising their warehousing, preparing orders and shipping them to stores.

There is a Supplier Workplace Code of Conduct, which includes banning child labour, forced labour and discrimination; ensuring work safety; respecting wages and decency; and offering the right to trade union membership.

The time it takes

Veja spends longer on designing its shoes than other big brands, taking the time that the manufacturing process really needs. The design ethos is to make trainers that should be timeless. Veja estimates that its trainers cost five times more to produce than other big-brand trainers. Part of this can be explained by the fact the trainers are made using fair trade and organic raw materials. Veja offers a more equitable arrangement for parties involved in the production chain than many other companies. And the trainer manufacturer invests in research and new technologies.

Veja initially offset this economic model by choosing not to advertise or market its goods as commercial orthodoxy would have insisted. This is why in the early days of the business, Emma Watson of Harry Potter fame stepped on to fashion catwalks wearing a pair of Veja trainers, as did other celebrity fans. Launched in 2005, Veja sold out of its first collection of 4,500 pairs of trainers. In 2018, Veja sold 1 million pairs. Initially, it was the design of the trainer that brought fame and the interest of the market. The company's world-making purpose was unknown. Since then, the world has shifted.

The growth and scale of the trainers business has been carefully and responsibly managed based on fair trade principles with Veja's suppliers. 'This rhythm of growth was human. That way you can avoid a lot of obstacles,' says Kopp. 'Beautiful things take time to make. We like to build the house brick by brick, built with love. We are more interested in the roots of the tree rather than in it growing fast and becoming weak.'

What world do you want to make?

The times have found us.

—

Thomas Paine

We need to reimagine the world we live in. Veja is an example of that reimagining. The trainer brand demonstrates how the values and intentions of businesses are changing. They are part of a revolutionary act of transforming in how we see the world, how we create and make products. Businesses like Veja serve a social purpose with hope and optimism. There are ways to design and make a business that can meet multiple goals. The making of profit through the exploitation of people or the earth's natural resources is simply bad business practice.

Leadership

When asked how he judges the rest of the fashion industry for what they do or don't do in terms of ethical manufacturing, Kopp replies that first he sees fashion as a mirror held up to society. I agree, so what do we see? There is a pause. Kopp then says that as a young man, he judged too much, but that was distracting. Today, he prefers to leave the judging to others and to get on with what he does best: building a beautiful business as best he can, with the skills he has to offer. His biggest challenge is building a good team, the right team, which is rich in ideas and diversity. Kopp says, 'The greatest success of Veja is the team — it represents extraordinary diversity.'

Master and commander

Veja is 100 per cent owned by its two founders. Kopp argues that too much is made about money, investment and rapid growth. This obsession with speed creates a false sense of urgency. 'I don't like urgency as that is when you make mistakes,' says Kopp.

The mattering

For the founders of Veja, things matter: how are their trainers made? How much are labourers paid? How much does an organic cotton producer earn? What are the chemicals used in a pair of Veja trainers? Asking and answering these questions has taken them down the path of transformation. This covers regeneration, the circular economy, leadership as generosity and responsibility for 'The Total'— the concept of what we take, make and waste.

Look at the experience of the product itself, the quality, the elegance, the language the company uses, the transparency, the traceability and the making of a product they would happily sell to their friends and families. Did they and do they enjoy the process? Every day brings complex challenges, but the satisfaction of doing good in business must be priceless. That is what money can't buy—a legacy worth leaving behind.

You can now buy Veja trainers in retailers around the world. When you are out and about, look down at what people are wearing on their feet. As my millennial friend said to me, 'We want the cool thing and we want the right thing.'

Climeworks: doing something truly beautiful

The inspiration for the Swiss company Climeworks goes back 20 years. The two co-founders, Christoph Gebald and Jan Wurzbacher, met serendipitously on their first day of university at the Swiss Federal Institute of Technology in Zürich. The two engineers discovered a shared love for alpine sports. While staying in Chamonix in France on a three-month skiing holiday, they experienced first-hand the rapid retreat of glaciers, representing the effects of climate change. Standing in their ski gear, the engineers looked at a 50m ladder used by mountaineers to climb down to the glacier. The locals explained that two metres had to be added to the ladder every year. The engineers felt they could not walk away from such evidence.

But in their plan to build a business addressing climate change, they encountered a challenge. Scientific studies indicate that by 2050, the world will need to remove 10 billion tons of carbon dioxide from the atmosphere every year. This is not so much a question of reduction; it is about taking back the carbon warming the planet. This is why Gebald and Wurzbacher wanted to develop a technology that could capture carbon dioxide (CO_2) directly from the air. Their ambition was that air-captured CO_2 could be recycled, for example in heating commercial greenhouses, used as a raw material, or completely removed from the air by safely storing it.

Critics said it could not be done, and would never be commercially viable. And yet Climeworks proved that it could work. Wurzbacher explains how the Swiss company's approach links with current investing practices and timelines. 'I believe a big problem in the financing of sustainable projects is the time horizon. The typical venture capital or even private equity model has a fund which you fill up, you invest, then after five, seven or even ten years you have to repay the fund,' he says. 'A typical venture capital fund is not the best partner to scale businesses focused on regeneration and industrial innovation. We are fortunate to have shareholders with a very long horizon line. They are looking to build up a new industry. Climeworks investors are entrepreneurs, Swiss, German, some slightly further afield, who share this long-term vision.'

Innovative technology

Now that Climeworks has developed a technology called direct air capture, it has established ten commercial plants. The most important of these was set up as a joint venture with an Icelandic company called Carbfix, an expert in the rapid underground mineralisation of carbon dioxide. The Carbfix process centres around the Hellisheiði geothermal power plant provides the renewable energy that is needed to run the Climeworks machines. It is one of the world's first carbon-negative plants, showing how we can go from the term 'net zero' to 'climate positive'.

Climeworks draws CO_2 from the atmosphere with its direct air capture machines. Carbfix then mixes this with water and pumps it deep underground. Through a process of natural mineralisation, the CO_2 reacts with the basalt rock and is converted into stone within a few years; it is returned safely to the earth. With the machine-based solution of Climeworks, the amount of CO_2 that has been turned into stone can be accurately measured.

We need people like these mechanical engineers because you can't do business on a dead planet. If ever a company needed to scale, it's this one.

The excitement of Wurzbacher is clear as he talks about what Climeworks' partner Carbfix has done in Iceland, where CO_2 is converted into stone. 'When you are looking at CO_2 storage, there are many questions: Is it safe? Will the carbon release itself? Conventional CO_2 storage is safe and well understood,' he says. 'But I couldn't think of anything better than turning it into stone and storing it a thousand metres underground. It works so well we have plans to scale this around the world together.'

Currently, Climeworks is building its next plant in Iceland, which will extract 4,000 tons of CO_2 a year, then scale by a factor of 25 to 100,000 tons. Towards the mid-2020s, the Swiss company plans to reach 1 million tons. This could offer a scale-up path where, every two to three years, Climeworks has a new generation of technology with higher efficiency and lower costs; summing up how you can build a business by harnessing the potential of innovative technology.

The circular economy

Climeworks helps us to understand the importance of the circular economy. Wurzbacher believes that in the next five years, no CEO of a large corporation will get away with not having a climate target and a larger sustainability target at the top of their agenda. This takes us back to what people in wider society are asking for. 'The only way we can move forward is thinking in circles,' he says, 'acting as a circular economy, and telling better stories and enabling people to meaningfully contribute.'

Wurzbacher goes on to say that the battles they are facing are stories about belief. So, one should not tell the story in a way that suggests we need to stop doing things. Instead, we must build a positive narrative. 'Every story we are telling is around how we can do something, how we can act. There is technology that can solve many problems. I am a skier and a windsurfer, and I want to continue doing these things. Sometimes, I need to get on a plane to go somewhere, and I hope I can still do this but in a sustainable way.'

This is where the idea of designing something truly beautiful comes in. Wurzbacher explains that beauty can be found in a solution that has a long-term foundation. 'Beauty is something that I could imagine sustains us well into the future. We could build a rocket which has a finite amount of energy which burns, then has to eventually come back to earth,' he says. 'Or, we could build a solar-powered ship that could in theory sail around the world forever. You could even have a team on board that could maintain and repair the ship — that is beautiful.' That has echoes of the ideas of John Ruskin.

The power of people

Everyone can contribute, according to Wurzbacher. 'This is something that has been on my mind,' he says. 'What I increasingly see is people asking us, how can we contribute?' He reflects on how the task can seem insurmountable for an individual, but can be overcome as a collective: the most powerful tool to trigger action is through everyone doing their bit. He adds, 'If every employee asked their employer to become sustainable, they would have to do it ... We have welcomed people approaching us.'

The Climeworks co-founder continues: 'I believe in the power of people and the power of the perception of people. Because so many approached us, we found a way to empower them to contribute to climate change and CO_2 reduction in particular.' They have introduced an element of sustainability to their innovative business model by creating a service where people could contribute to the process of drawing CO_2 out of the atmosphere.

'We were overwhelmed by the reaction, with no marketing at all. We are mechanical engineers. Our business model was, we sell machines; it didn't work that way. It is not the typical business model of a company to buy a machine that takes CO_2 out of the atmosphere,' says Wurzbacher. 'What we realised is a company has a climate target. People possess a desire to act on climate change. They don't have the capability, infrastructure and hardware to do so, but they might love it as a service. Now, we are offering carbon removal to corporate and private clients as a service.'

The adventurous engineer has high aspirations for the future. 'I hope we can scale this not only for revenue, but because we can then affect policy. If one day we had a million pioneers doing this with us it would be important, not only to generate cash and scale our technology, but more importantly to create momentum for change at a policy level. What we are building is a new industry, a new eco-system.'

Values

Looking at the foundational values of this book — beauty, nature, biomimicry, design, values and metrics, and governance — Climeworks is doing something truly beautiful. The Swiss company is working on behalf of two key stakeholders: society and the earth. The co-founders are defined by their values-based worldview. Their desire is to bring more responsible and ecologically restorative ways of doing business into the world.

The business pays respect to nature and accepts a responsibility to regenerate the earth. This takes us back to the deepest relationship that humanity has with the natural world. In the table of value creation metrics of a regenerative economy presented earlier in the book (see p. 24), Climeworks is contributing, not taking. The company responds to John Ruskin's maxim that we need to focus on things that will sustain us for an eternity.

Adopting the principle that nature is the best designer we have, Climeworks has applied lessons of biomimicry. Inspired by her principles, the business embraces the circular economy in working with a long timeframe. Often this is where pioneering technological innovation falls down, as investors make short-term demands for success. In that sense, the founders of Climeworks are being good ancestors, creating a legacy for future generations. Without a doubt, Gebald and Wurzbacher are resourceful human beings, as well as being leaders who have a compelling story that inspires and motivates.

Climeworks demonstrates an ability to envisage a novel solution to a complicated problem, with a supreme act of design engineering. My belief is that great design is perseverance fuelled by optimism. My friend Laurence John, co-founder and CEO of ctrlio and a pioneer in his own right, said to me, 'Beauty is like a gene; genes don't do anything, but nothing happens without them, whereas protein does the work — show people the protein.' Here, Climeworks is doing beauty.

The Hellisheiði ON geothermal power plant, Iceland

7
'Re':
a manifesto
for the future

Another world is not only possible,
she is on her way. On a quiet day,
I can hear her breathing.

—

Arundhati Roy

This book is about what makes us human, what makes us whole, and how we build a world worth living in, not just for us, but for all those who will come after. We all need to create a legacy. My hope is that this book has inspired and enabled readers, weaving together the practical with the soulful. Because otherwise why are we here, and what does all this effort mean?

In my previous book, *Do Design*, I spoke of the philosophy of 'ing', suggesting beauty was a verb, not a noun, because verbs describe the animacy of life. My intention is to invite the possibility that in everything we do, all our practices are action-based, where beauty is always present. By 'doing beauty', we individually and collectively can do good in business. Now, I would like to move to a manifesto for the future.

From 'ing' to 'Re'

This manifesto is founded in the philosophy of 'Re'. The concept of 'Re' is the foundation upon which we must rebuild a world that we would all want to live in and describe as beautiful. 'Re' is for regeneration. 'Re' takes us beyond the mindset of sustainability. It offers us something richer, more fulfilling; it is the universal path leading towards the flourishing of all life.

Work needs to be done if we want beauty to be our homecoming. Regeneration is in the business of creating abundance and restoring dignity for all. Over the coming years, it will be our work to bestow gifts upon the world in the same way as nature bestows her gifts on us. Our 'ings' must be acts of reciprocity.

Nature writer Robin Wall Kimmerer has written a book called *Braiding Sweetgrass* in which she explains why this is true: 'Pioneer communities, just like pioneer plant communities, have an important role in regeneration, but they are not sustainable in the long run. When they reach the edge of easy, energy, balance and renewal are the only way forward, wherein there is a reciprocal cycle between early and late successional systems, each opening the door for the other. The old growth forest is as stunning in its elegance of function as in its beauty.'

Our work must build from nature. We can learn to be inspired by her design model; we must use design as a civilising force. Consider what might happen if all the people that code in this world coded for beauty, designed for beautiful outcomes: what world would we be creating? Begin by reconnecting yourself to a set of values, which frame the pathway of bringing the good into your daily life. These values are concerned with compassion, empathy, reciprocity, generosity and respecting each other.

Beauty: the ultimate metric

Our responsibility is also to ensure we create ways in which we can measure the return to equilibrium between our economy, our ecology and our community. Equilibrium demands we address scale and growth. We must design businesses for scale as nature intended, rather than for infinite growth. Think about how water flows from a source, from a spring to a river and an estuary to an ocean — all are connected, all are needed. Growth needs to be circular, and reciprocal.

If by scaling we take more than we are able to replace, or we create suffering, then we should not be forcing the scaling of the business. If we are to grow, then it should be done so that growth feels inevitable and continues to create abundance in the world. Does the world need us, and does the world need more of us?

Leading with generosity

In regenerating our world, we need leadership to be rooted in wisdom. This is leadership steeped in values with the desire to be a good ancestor. Your work, to create a legacy for future generations, is your gift to the world. Approaching leadership with a sense of generosity is the way forward. This is about knowing how to nurture joyful working cultures and building a place where people love the work they do. Beautiful things can only ever be made with love.

A beautiful leader takes full responsibility for themselves, developing their own practice to restore and regenerate the economy and the environment. Otherwise, how could you lead with generosity, compassion and empathy?

The telling of stories

Leadership requires you to be a powerful storyteller, firing people's imaginations and inviting others to draw from the deepest wells of their creativity. Make no mistake, words create worlds; language is generative. Stories have potency, describing how we can be in the world. We can see what stories visualise and the ideas they contain. From a story perspective, if we cannot describe a new destination that excites, motivates and evokes a yearning in people, we will never get there.

Consider the climate crisis: we are all doomed. How do you feel? Excited, motivated, ready to give your all to the task ahead? Unlikely. But what if we think about climate change as an opportunity, offering the means to rethink, redesign and remake our world? Some might describe this as utopian, but we don't get to create or discover anything without belief and optimism, even under the most perilous conditions.

Enduring stories carry an irreducible truth and symbolism, standing impervious to time. Narratives call us to listen. They shape our beliefs. The stories we tell now must describe our quest for regeneration. If our stories fail to inspire who we want to become, then we fail too. But when we do succeed, our best stories inspire a desire for a better world, generating the capacity to make great things that transcend generations, even centuries.

So, finally, my gaze turns to you as I offer an invitation and a challenge. Start to build and lead your business by using the principles of leadership and the 13 design questions asked in this book. Consider what they might inspire in you and your organisation to create a business invested in rebuilding, restoring, redesigning, recreating, recycling and rewilding, in so doing, bestowing gifts that our world needs.

Appendix:
50 beautiful businesses

Early on I somehow understood that an idea
can be something very beautiful, as beautiful
as an object or anything else. And once you
understand that, you are open to things and
maybe search for them.

—

Daniel Marzona

Over the last few years, I have been researching companies
that show how we can live and work with more grace
and dignity, how we can better serve society and how to
regenerate our planet. Evoking the ethos of craftsmanship,
these companies are the makers of civilisation, creating
conditions that are conducive for life to thrive.

They represent different aspects of scale, and they
demonstrate that growth needs time, care, love and
attention — growth is not infinite. They represent the
truth that life thrives when existing in a diverse ecosystem:
this is nature's design model. All of these companies
(and I've gone so far as to include some cities and even
a pioneering country) show leadership vested with the
belief of doing good in business, while exemplifying
quality in thought and action. They all speak the language
of beauty.

What follows is a brief description of each company.
Look at this as a learning laboratory to test your own ideas
on how you might make your business more beautiful.
(Of course, not all of these businesses will stand the test
of time. Some may not even survive the turbulence of
2020, but if they do then it's a wonderful representation
of resilience if nothing else).

1. Veja

Veja makes trainers. Apart from the trend where everybody wants this style of trainer, this French brand makes them by using a more transparent supply chain and more sustainable materials than many of its competitors. Brands are increasingly being held to account by their customers, who want all the style and none of their ugly secrets.
project.veja-store.com

2. Páramo

Páramo is one of the few PFC-free outdoor brands currently on the market. Páramo uses an alternative fabric technology, and the company ensures all its garments can be recycled. PFCS, or perfluorinated compounds, are a staple in many fabrics used for outdoor clothing. They are popular with the industry's big brands because they create a porous outer layer that allows impermeable, waterproof materials to breathe, while making surfaces repel water and oil.
paramo-clothing.com

3. What3Words

What3Words is a navigation and geolocation tool that divides the world into 3m by 3m squares. Take a moment to think about the scale of the concept. Nothing compares, no postcode system is even close. Some countries do not even use postal codes or are so vast that no current system possesses such location granularity. Each square has a three-word address that will never change in What3Words. The tool can help with finding friends at a remote location or at a festival of 50,000 people, sending urgent humanitarian aid or even saving lives in remote parts of the world. What3Words offers geolocation precision when you need it most.
what3words.com

4. Naim Audio

Naim Audio has been designing and producing handmade music systems from its base in Salisbury in the UK since it was incorporated in 1973. The audio firm now exports to more than 45 countries and has more than 60 products in the range. This is a story of quality, in this instance the quality of sound, the quality of the experience and how that can change how you feel. But it is more than that. Naim builds its HiFi systems for lifelong use.
naimaudio.com

5. Worldreader

Every child deserves the right to knowledge, which can be accessed through reading. With low-cost technology, culturally relevant digital books and a network of corporate and non-profit partners, Worldreader is helping millions of children in Africa to read more. The organisation's mobile application enables you to read e-books in various languages, from across the world. It's a remarkable story that shows how technology can scale for good.
worldreader.org

6. Museum Beyeler

Julien Robson, a curator of contemporary art, has been in more museums around the world than most. I asked him which was the most beautiful. With no hesitation, Julien replied, 'The Museum Beyeler in Switzerland, designed by Renzo Piano.' Why is a gallery in this list? Because art is part of life. Artists are the cultural astronauts of our world. We all need to be inspired and challenged.
fondationbeyeler.ch

7. The Santa Cruz Guitar Company

The Santa Cruz Guitar Company, founded in 1976, hand-builds steel-string guitars. They are works of true craftsmanship. This company cares about where its materials come from, and its dedication to making the very best guitars is evident. There is a wonderful video (see link in Resources), which founders and CEOS should watch as a provocation as to how the ethos of craftsmanship applied to the world of work can be life-enhancing. In the film, the founder Richard Hoover says of the people in his company, 'We work for meaning.'
santacruzguitar.com

8. Waugh Thistleton Architects

Waugh Thistleton Architects, based in Shoreditch, is a pioneer in the field of tall timber buildings, and a practice focused on designing and building sustainable homes. The firm is one of the world's leading companies in using engineered timber in construction.
waughthistleton.com

9. Gränsfors Bruk

Gränsfors Bruk makes some of the best axes in the world. Their way of creating value — not only in the product itself but throughout the company — is their sustained focus on simplicity. Their highly-refined designs are fit for purpose and each axe maker is rewarded for quality over quantity. The company honours the materials it uses, the people who make them, and the people who use them.
gransforsbruk.com

10. Interface

Interface makes carpet tiles and flooring products. The company reached its goal of becoming carbon-neutral in

2019 by completely redesigning its supply chain and production processes with technological innovation and creative ambition. Interface has now embarked on its next mission, called Climate Takeback, to become a regenerative business. The company wants to restore the planet and leave a positive impact. It's never too late to press the reset button and become a pioneer.
interface.com

11. Florian Gadsby

Florian Gadsby is a ceramicist based in north London. His work represents the ancient tradition of pottery and craftsmanship. He began as an apprentice to Ken Matsuzaki in Mashiko, Japan, so his work carries that influence, both in form and glazing. The handmade is still needed in this world. There is a reason for the resurgence of craft-based products, in terms of the making and the using. The great Japanese craftsman Soetsu Yanagi discovered beauty in utilitarian objects of everyday life: 'There is no greater opportunity for appreciating beauty than through its use in our daily lives.'
floriangadsby.com

12. Xero

Xero is an accountancy software platform that serves small and medium-sized enterprises (SMEs). Accounting is one of those things we all have to do. The process can be ugly. Or, it could be beautiful, as you can see in a beautifully designed business such as this one. The company takes one of life's absolute truths, taxes (not death), and delivers a service that is life-simplifying, with an elegant user experience (UX) and business model.
xero.com

13. Brunello Cucinelli

Brunello Cucinelli has been making clothes very successfully since 1978. While he sells luxury cashmere jumpers, he has an ethical business approach. He pays his staff more than the average wage for their jobs and insists they work no longer than eight-and-a-half hours a day. An advocate of sustainable business, he has a long history of philanthropic activities. Before the company's flotation in 2011, it invested 20 per cent of its earnings into the family foundation. He runs an oversubscribed craft school. Cucinelli says, 'Everything in this business has to be gracious. Profit is the gift when creation is perfect. I would like to make a profit using ethics, dignity and morals. Of course, I believe in a form of capitalism. I would just like it to be more human.'
brunellocucinelli.com

14. Good Hotel

Good Hotel give jobs to long-term unemployed people, enabling them to build careers in hospitality. This is a business with a mission to finance an education programme in Guatemala for low-income families. A friend stayed recently at its London site; he said its staff were amazing. Each hotel uses local resources and ingredients. Simple, great design makes wellbeing a part of the offering. They have a sign in the restaurant / lobby that says, 'Create Beauty. Do Good.'
goodhotellondon.com

15. The Hogeweyk

The Hogeweyk is a village-style neighbourhood in the small town of Weesp, near Amsterdam, created in 2009. With a gated model, it has been designed as a pioneering care facility for elderly people with dementia. Here you can do what you once did, live a life, whatever that looks like,

as normally as possible, while receiving 24 / 7 care from trained staff. Residents can move around and interact with the world, and consequently may require less medication. To solve a complex challenge such as dementia, you can find a beautiful way — it just requires compassion.
dementiavillage.com

16. Folkhem

Folkhem is a building company that makes housing only from wood. Folkhem is one of the first companies to register an EPD® of a building in this international system. The Environmental Product Declaration (EPD®) is an independently verified and registered document that communicates transparent and comparable information about the environmental impact of products across their life cycles.
folkhem.se

17. Åarhus

Åarhus is home to an automated multi-storey car park, which is one of the first buildings of its type in Denmark. Multi-storey car parks have many issues, such as the queuing to get in and out at peak times, personal safety in the evening or early morning and levels of crime. How do you solve the complex problem of city parking? This car park in Åarhus is an example of automation at work, which elegantly solves many complex problems. This shows a choreography of use at an urban scale.

18. Falcon Coffees

Falcon Coffees is a coffee trading house that sources green coffee from 18 producing countries and works with coffee-roasting companies all over the world. The company buys coffee from rural farming communities in some of the poorest economies in the world. The coffee buyer's mission is to create a fairer economy in the growing of coffee, establishing a more resilient and regenerative supply chain.

falconcoffees.com

19. Finisterre

Finisterre produces clothes for the outdoors that are fit for purpose and makes sustainability its way of life. The company is committed to minimising environmental impact. Central to this mission is circular sourcing, which includes renewable and recyclable textiles and biodegradable natural fibres and finishes. Finisterre also produces a fully recyclable wetsuit.

finisterre.com

20. Fairphone

Fairphone has a slogan of being the phone that cares for people and planet. The Dutch firm has a mission to improve the conditions of the people who make phones, and responsibly sources materials. Because how it's made matters.

fairphone.com

21. Piet Oudolf

Garden designer Piet Oudolf is one of the gardening greats. The man behind the New Perennial movement applies naturalistic planting to all his projects. Gardens are restorative. We tend our gardens with care and love. They are a metaphor for selfless giving and what one receives in return — enduring satisfaction.

oudolf.com

22. M-Kopa Solar

The M-Kopa solar lighting and charging system works on a pay-as-you-go business model. At the time of writing, it has reached more than 750,000 homes. The largest off-grid solar operator in sub-Saharan Africa, it offers clean power to consumers in Kenya, Uganda and Tanzania for a daily fee. M-Kopa's mission is to upgrade the lives of people on a low income. We all need the light after dark.
m-kopa.com

23. Alison Brooks Architects

Alison Brooks Architects is a practice that believes architecture should reclaim the language of beauty for buildings, cities and towns. Alison Brooks's work in architecture is based on four ideals: authenticity, generosity, civicness and beauty.
alisonbrooksarchitects.com

24. Vitsoe

Vitsoe makes shelving and furniture, designed by Dieter Rams, using material that is fully recyclable. The company designs thoughtfully, responsibly and intelligently, as you can see in its furniture. Based in Leamington Spa, the factory has been designed and built to the highest specification. The company works on the principle that its products are made to live very long lives.
vitsoe.com

25. Sven Cycles

Sven Cycles has established a reputation as a respected builder of high-quality bicycles from its workshop in Weymouth, Dorset. The company has received numerous Bespoked Bicycle Show awards for its work.
svencycles.com

26. The Oxford Community Energy Co-op

The Oxford Community Energy Co-operative is about 90 minutes' drive away from Toronto in Canada. It stemmed from a local community's initiative to raise CA$9 million to fund a wind farm with ten Senvion MM92 wind turbines. By late 2016, it was announced that the turbines were generating 18 megawatts of electricity and powering 6,700 homes, free from emissions. The co-operative venture is creating jobs locally, and people who are members of the co-op are making money from their investment.
oxford-cec.ca

27. Rotterdam

The Netherlands' second city, and Europe's biggest port, is now attracting designers, artists and architects, who are reshaping the Dutch city into an epicentre of urban innovation. The local council has pursued a vision for the city's development over the last 40 years to turn it into a truly public domain. One hub for innovative companies is BlueCity, located in a former swimming pool.
bluecity.nl

28. Helsinki Central Library Oodi

How do you design for community at a city scale? You build a multi-purpose library. Oodi takes the form of a vast interior town square and open space, built upon a foundation of learning, inclusivity, community and culture. This is Finland at its very best. What is a library? What does it hold? Who does it serve? Why does it matter? These are all design considerations.
oodihelsinki.fi

29. Knepp Castle Estate

Knepp Farm is a 3,500-acre farm in West Sussex, barely 45 miles from London. Once a conventional dairy and arable operation, the farm was financially on its knees until it was slowly regenerated in a rewilding process. This encouraged the return of insects, animals and birds, which are now thriving, even the rare turtle dove. The estate has turned into a profitable business and a demonstration of how critical biodiversity is for all life. Knepp now makes its money from eco-tourism, a farm shop selling high-grade organic meat reared on the estate, upmarket camping and the rental of agricultural buildings for businesses — which has created 200 jobs.
knepp.co.uk

30. Project Drawdown

Project Drawdown, founded by Paul Hawken, is one of the most comprehensive plans proposed to reverse global warming. The project's mission is to help the world reach a 'drawdown' point at which levels of greenhouse gases in the atmosphere stop climbing and begin to decline, preventing catastrophic climate change. The project outlines the 100 most substantive solutions to tackle climate change.
drawdown.org

31. World Central Kitchen

World Central Kitchen, founded by Michelin-Starred chef José Andrés, set up a remarkable restaurant in Puerto Rico, serving millions of meals to starving people after Hurricane Maria devastated the island in September 2017. The company's mission is to provide food-related means, resources, education and first-responder help for communities around the world.
wck.org

32. Commonland

Commonland works with large-scale landscape initiatives. Its holistic approach to landscape restoration starts by understanding an area's economics, local leadership, capacity for ecological restoration and land tenure. The company explores the potential of regenerative business cases, which can drive what is termed '4 Returns', a holistic framework for landscape restoration at scale.
commonland.com

33. Patagonia

Patagonia manufactures outdoor clothing and is in the business of saving our planet. The company has been a pioneer of encouraging us to think about the world in which we live. Since its inception, Patagonia has been an activist business, educating people about their relationship to the earth and their responsibilities towards the planet.
patagonia.com

34. ReTuna

ReTuna is a shopping mall in Eskilstuna, about 70 miles west of Stockholm in Sweden, where a wide selection of retailers sell upcycled, reused and recycled goods, ranging from second-hand clothes to bicycles, building materials and furniture. This is every eco-warrior's Valhalla.
retuna.se

35. Zero-waste Retail

Zero-waste retail is growing as people become increasingly alarmed by the level of plastics in our oceans and microplastics in their lungs. Retailers in this field include the zero-waste shop Natural Weigh in Wales; the zero-waste supermarket Clean Kilo in Birmingham, England;

the organic supermarket OHNE in Germany; and the franchise The Source Bulk Foods, which has more than 50 shops across Australia and the UK. These are all responses to how people want to bring change to the world we live in. Thinking about what we make and why we make must become the norm. Zero waste is good design. *naturalweigh.co.uk, thecleankilo.co.uk, ohne-laden.shop, thesourcebulkfoods.co.uk*

36. Friluftssykehuset Foundation Charity

The Friluftssykehuset Foundation is a charitable foundation, built in partnership with the Norwegian architecture firm Snøhetta, which has created Outdoor Care Retreats known as *'friluftssykehuset'*. The term derives from the Norwegian concept of *'friluftsliv'* — the importance of spending time in nature — combined with the Norwegian word for hospital, *'sykehus'*. Research shows the benefits of convalescing in nature as it can help people to recover more quickly after operations.

37. Produttori del Barbaresco

Produttori del Barbaresco produces two of Italy's greatest red wines, Barolo and Barbaresco. The winery co-operative was founded in 1958, although its roots go back to 1894, before it was closed down by Mussolini in the 1930s. Produttori del Barbaresco was among the first wineries in Italy to pay farmers for quality over quantity and continues to set some of the highest standards of winemaking for any co-operative in the world.
produttoridelbarbaresco.com

38. La Marzocco

La Marzocco was founded in Florence in 1927 and is a family-owned company to this day, manufacturing some of the best hand-built coffee machines in the world. Aspects of its policy are a total devotion to its people, a focus on quality and an emphasis on innovation.
international.lamarzocco.com

39. Otter Surfboards

Otter Surfboards in Cornwall makes wooden surfboards from managed local forests. They are the product of the shared twin passions of surfing and fine woodworking that drive the workshop, with a strong nod to the planet that we live on. The company was founded by craftsman and designer James Otter.
ottersurfboards.co.uk

40. New Zealand

In 2019, New Zealand unveiled its first 'wellbeing budget' and instructed its ministries to design policies to improve the wellbeing of its citizens. In the next fiscal year, all of the country's non-core spending must be oriented to one of five government priorities: improving mental health, reducing child poverty, addressing the inequalities faced by indigenous Maori and Pacific Islands people, transitioning to a low-emission, sustainable economy and thriving in a digital age. And to measure success, the government will track non-traditional indicators, such as perceived environmental quality and sense of belonging.

41. The Bristol Bike Project

James Lucas and his friend Colin Fan came up with a fragment of an idea for the Bristol Bike Project when making a cycle trip through Norway. The Bristol Bike Project helps

people from all walks of life to get on two wheels to travel to and from work. Through the people they connect with every day, they nurture the idea of a life in motion, which has the potential to transform a community.
thebristolbikeproject.org

42. icebreaker

icebreaker takes fibre from nature that is designed to keep alive an animal, the merino sheep, and turns it into 'high performance' natural clothing to keep humans alive in nature. Started in 1994, icebreaker was a pioneer in developing a merino layering system for wearing in the outdoors. icebreaker was also the first outdoor clothing company to source merino wool directly from farmers through a system started in 1997.
icebreaker.com

43. Bolt Threads

Bolt Threads addresses the problem that the manufacturing of textiles is a great source of pollution. The company has developed two innovative materials and production processes: Microsilk, inspired by the properties of spider silk, and Mylo, a leather material made from mycelium, part of a fungus. Bolt's materials are produced with less waste and fewer natural resources in an attempt to reduce environmental impact. Bolt envisions a world where we don't have to deplete or pollute our forests, oceans and rivers to benefit from their natural secrets.
boltthreads.com

44. Kew Gardens Seed Bank

Within the vaults of the Millennium Seed Bank at Kew Gardens' Wakehurst site in West Sussex is a growing collection of seeds, which represents one of the greatest concentrations of living seed-plant diversity on the planet. The Millennium Seed Bank is a global resource for conservation and education about the sustainable use of plants.

kew.org

45. Atelier Luma

Atelier Luma is a think tank, a production workshop and a learning network of the Luma Foundation. Situated in Arles, in the Camargue region of France, Atelier Luma is creating sustainable ways of using the natural and cultural resources of the bioregion by using design as a tool for transition.

atelier-luma.org

46. Rotor Deconstruction

Rotor Deconstruction does not use wood from living trees, but salvages materials from condemned buildings. On average, each resident in Belgium throws away around half a ton of household rubbish per year, which, added together, is about the same as the amount of new material the country imports. To achieve a sense of equilibrium, Rotor Deconstruction is recycling and upcycling building materials for reuse.

rotordc.com

47. Copenhagen

The capital of Denmark has set itself the goal of becoming the world's first carbon-neutral city by 2025, with 100 new wind turbines; a 20 per cent reduction in heat and commercial electricity consumption; 75 per cent of all journeys to be made by bike, on foot or by public transport; becoming a world leader in converting organic waste into biogas; 60,000 square metres of new solar panels; and 100 per cent of the city's heating requirements to be met by renewables. Cities can be leaders, too.

48. Kongō Gumi

Founded in 578, Japanese construction company Kongō Gumi operated for an extraordinary 1,400 years until it became a subsidiary of Takamatsu in 2006. It specialises in the repair of traditional Buddhist temples using time-honoured practices and materials. Read more here: *worksthatwork.com/3/kongo-gumi*

49. Justdiggit

Justdiggit makes dry land green again by inspiring and activating farmers in Africa, bringing a positive impact to people, nature and climate change. This restores degraded landscapes by combining traditional techniques with new technology and a strong communication approach. *justdiggit.org*

50.

Write your name here.

For love to return to the world, beauty must first return, else we love the world only as a moral duty. Clean it up, preserve its nature, exploit it less. If love depends on beauty, then beauty comes first.

—

James Hillman, *The Practice of Beauty*

Resources

Read

After Nature
W.G. Sebald

The Art of Communicating
Thich Nhat Hanh

The Art of Loving
Erich Fromm

The Beauty of Everyday Things
Soetsu Yanagi

Biomimicry
Janine Benyus

Braiding Sweetgrass
Robin Wall Kimmerer

The Craftsman
Richard Sennett

Dare to Lead
Brené Brown

Design as an Attitude
Alice Rawsthorn

Divine Beauty
John O'Donohue

Drawdown
Paul Hawken

Growth: From Microorganisms to Megacities
Vaclav Smil

Ideals Then Ideas
Alison Brooks

Silence in the Age of Noise
Erling Kagge

The Sovereignty of Good
Iris Murdoch

The Spell of the Sensuous: Perception and language in a more-than-human world
David Abram

Studio Olafur Eliasson: The Kitchen
Olafur Eliasson

Timeless Beauty
John Lane

The Wandering Maker
Machiel Spaan

Wilding
Isabella Tree

Watch

2040
Directed by Damon Gameau
An inspirational journey to discover what the future could look like if we simply embraced the best solutions that exist today

Anselm Kiefer: Remembering the Future
BBC Imagine series

Rams
Directed by Gary Hustwit
A documentary about industrial designer Dieter Rams

Richard Hoover Among Giants Santa Cruz Guitar Company
vimeo.com/95917765

Tashi and the Monk
Directed by Andrew Hinton and Johnny Burke
vimeo.com/95735800

Things to do

Go for a walk every day; walk in nature for at least an hour

All meetings should be walking meetings

About the Author

Alan Moore is a designer and business innovator on a mission to help businesses discover their own unique beauty.

Working directly with companies and organisations, Alan mentors teams and individuals, delivers inspirational leadership programmes, and advises clients on how to design and build a regenerative business. Alan has shared his knowledge in the form of board and advisory positions, and has taught in institutions including MIT, the Sloan School of Management and INSEAD.

Alan is the author of four books on creativity and business transformation, including *Do Design: Why beauty is key to everything* (Do Books, 2016). He has spoken at The Do Lectures, SXSW and the Hay Literary Festival and has featured in the media.

Alan still works as an artist. Every day, he tries to lead his life as beautifully as he possibly can.

You can find out more on his website: *beautiful.business*

Thanks

I have been blessed with many wonderful conversations, experiences and helping hands as I have written this book. To all the business leaders, spiritual leaders, founders, craftspeople, environmental activists, architects and academics who have given their time so generously, I am truly grateful. To Liz and John, Mia and Jess Harrison: a big thank you for lending me your splendid Dutch barge, where I could write in peace, looking out on the River Cam. To Richard Pleasants, for being a trusted advisor and co-conspirator. To Tess Pleasants, for your kindness and true friendship. To Mads Thimmer, CEO of Innovation Lab, thank you for riffing with me on the difference between the model of extractive vs. regenerative economics, and many other things besides. To Johnnie Moore for the creative input always challenging me to be my best. To Charlotte Lawrence for her support and feedback. To Julien Robson for your enduring love and friendship. To Nat Weiss for all help Stateside. To Julian Calverley, one of Britain's best landscape photographers and a lifelong friend. To Piper, my dog, and my walking and talking companion for 11 years, RIP. To the natural world for healing me, I could not have done it without you. Lastly, a great big thank you to my publisher, Miranda West, and the team at Do Books.

Index

Books in the series

Also available

BooK Co

Available in print, digital and audio formats from booksellers or via our website: **thedobook.co**

To hear about events and forthcoming titles, you can find us on social media **@dobookco**, or subscribe to our newsletter